The Laughter Prescription

Cal and Rose Samra

WATERBROOK
PRESS

THE LAUGHTER PRESCRIPTION
PUBLISHED BY WATERBROOK PRESS
5446 North Academy Boulevard, Suite 200
Colorado Springs, Colorado 80918
A division of Random House, Inc.

For information about the Fellowship of Merry Christians and *The Joyful Noiseletter,* please call toll-free 1-800-877-2757 from 8 A.M. to 5 P.M. E.S.T. M-F or write: FMC, PO Box 895, Portage, MI 49081-0895. E-mail: JoyfulNZ@aol.com
Visit FMC's website: www.JoyfulNoiseletter.com

Library of Congress Cataloging-in-Publication Data
The laughter prescription / [compiled by] Cal and Rosa Samra.
        p.   cm.
     ISBN 1-57856-286-4
        1. Health—Religious aspects—Christianity Humor.   2. Christian life
Humor.   3. Christianity Humor.   I. Samra, Cal.   II. Samra, Rose.
     PN6231.H38L385   1999
     610´.2´07—dc21   99-33685
                                                                          CIP

Printed in the United States of America
1999—First Edition

10 9 8 7 6 5 4 3 2 1

A merry heart doeth good like a medicine;
but a broken spirit drieth the bones.

—PROVERBS 17:22 (KJV)

PREFACE

"My friends Erma Bombeck and Art Buchwald have done far more for the health of humanity than Madame Curie or Dr. Christiaan Barnard," says cartoonist Bil Keane, creator of "The Family Circus," America's number-one cartoon panel.

Keane, a consulting editor to *The Joyful Noiseletter*, is a longtime believer in the healing power of humor. "One of the best ways to deal with stress," he says, "is to cultivate a sense of humor. He who laughs lasts!"

From time to time, a well-known comedian has confessed his belief that laughter has kept him living to a ripe old age. Consider George Burns, Red Skelton, Bob Hope, Henny Youngman, Milton Berle, and Danny Thomas.

Danny Thomas said, "Anytime I'm feeling old and down, I use laughter like a prescription. I laugh at life's problems and keep going."

Turning ninety-five, Bob Hope told *TV Guide* the secret to his longevity: "Laughter is it. Laughter is therapy—an instant vacation."

A recent study of one hundred centenarians by Harvard Medical School scientists found that they "were generally optimistic, use humor often, and in most cases, were funny."

"If it's sanity you're after," said Henry Rutherford Elliott, "there's no prescription like laughter."

—CAL AND ROSE SAMRA
EDITORS, *THE JOYFUL NOISELETTER*

A listener called in this story on Rev. Ron Lengwin's Sunday night talk show "Amplify" on Radio Station KDKA, Pittsburgh:

There used to be a popular restaurant in Pittsburgh called Captain Cook's. The owner, Barney Cook, was a real clown and cut-up. He was always playing practical jokes and cheering everybody up. Barney had a loudspeaker and would announce every customer's name as they came in.

One day, one of Barney's friends, Joe the mailman, stopped in. While he was eating dinner, he suddenly slumped over on the floor. Joe's face turned blue, and he was gasping for breath, like he was having a heart attack.

Everybody panicked. People were running around calling for a doctor, a nurse, and an ambulance. Barney calmly told everyone to move aside. He got down on his hands and knees and whispered in the man's ear: "Joe, can you hear me?"

"Yeah, I can hear you," Joe replied weakly.

"Have you paid your check?" Barney asked.

Joe started laughing—and laughing and laughing. A healthy color returned to his face, and by the time the ambulance arrived, Joe was up and assuring everyone he was feeling fine.

When humorist George Goldtrap was a Church of Christ minister in Madison, Tennessee, he was counseling a woman who was having marital problems.

"Does your husband believe in life after death?" Goldtrap asked.

"Hah! He doesn't even believe in life after supper," the woman said.

Three doctors died, went to heaven, and met St. Peter at the gates. St. Peter asked the first doctor why he thought he deserved to enter.

"I was a doctor with the Christian Medical and Dental Society," the physician replied. "Every year, I went to the Southwest for three weeks and treated the poor Native Americans free-of-charge."

"Welcome," said St. Peter. He asked the second doctor, "And what did you do?"

"I was a missionary in Africa for eleven years and worked in a hospital helping the tribes there," she replied.

"Enter into the joy of the Lord," St. Peter said. He turned to the third doctor and asked, "What did you do?"

"I was a doctor at an HMO."

"Come on in," St. Peter said, "but you can only stay three days."

While on a business trip, a Seventh-Day Adventist sales-man, who is a strict vegetarian, stopped off in a small town and telephoned his parents, who are not vegetarians. When his father answered the phone, the salesman said he would like to stop by for a visit. The father yelled to the mother: "The prodigal son is returning! Kill the fatted zucchini!"

"Could you talk to my niece, Job? She's going crazy because she has freckles."

William J. Murray, son of atheist Madalyn Murray O'Hair and author of *My Life without God*, became a Christian "because he couldn't stand the silences after the sneezes," according to Dean Edward Gaffney of the Valparaiso University Law School.

"Mirth is God's medicine. Everybody ought to bathe in it. Grim care, moroseness, anxiety—all this rust of life—ought to be scoured off by the oil of mirth."

—HENRY WARD BEECHER

A seminarian named Breeze
Weighed down by M.A.'s and Ph.D.'s,
Collapsed from the strain.
Said his doctor: "It's plain
You are killing yourself by degrees."

A certain doctor in Buffalo wondered why his practice was decreasing. He consulted a physician friend who agreed to spend a few days in the office and observe his methods.

After an hour, his friend had the answer. "Wilbur, you'll have to stop humming 'Nearer My God to Thee' when writing out a prescription."

—DR. FRANCIS LEO GOLDEN

Comedian Milton Berle relates that he visited comedian Jim Backus, the voice of the Mr. Magoo cartoon character, in the hospital a few months before Backus died. Berle told Backus jokes for two hours. Berle recalled: "As I left I turned to him and said, 'I hope you get better,' and he said, 'You too.'"

A burned-out assistant pastor was advised by his senior pastor to see a counselor. "Do you have trouble making decisions about your sermon themes?" the counselor asked.

"Well, yes…and no…," the pastor replied.

—VIA GEORGE GOLDTRAP, ORMOND-BY-THE-SEA, FLORIDA

A distraught man went to a psychiatrist and exclaimed, "Doctor, I believe that I am possessed by an evil spirit." After talking to the patient at some length, the psychiatrist said, "You do appear to have a problem. I'd like to see you again next Wednesday."

After a second session of psychotherapy, the psychiatrist pronounced his patient completely cured.

For the next nine months, the psychiatrist sent the man a monthly statement for his professional services, but the man wouldn't pay and refused to acknowledge the debt. Finally, the psychiatrist took the man to court and had him repossessed.

—REV. CHARLES B. HASTIE, MACKINAW CITY, MICHIGAN

A gambler died. The funeral was well attended by his professional friends. In the eulogy, the minister said: "Spike is not dead; he only sleeps."

From the rear of the chapel a man shouted: "I got a hundred that says he's dead."

—ARCHBISHOP JOHN L. MAY OF ST. LOUIS

"Through humor, you can soften some of the worst blows that life delivers. And once you find laughter, no matter how painful your situation might be, you can survive it."

—BILL COSBY

"You've confessed your sins with a contrite heart, Walter. Have confidence in the mercy of God."

An inexperienced preacher was conducting his first funeral. He solemnly pointed to the body in the coffin and declared: "What we have here is only a shell. The nut is already gone."

—George Goldtrap, Ormond-by-the-Sea, Florida

Two adjacent signs seen at the top of a large bookshelf in a Christian bookstore in Decatur, Illinois:

Women & Health	Men Death/Suffering/ Aging

DIETER'S PRAYER

Lord, grant me the strength
That I may not fall
Into the clutches of cholesterol.
The road to hell is paved with butter,
Cake is cursed, cream is awful,
And Satan is hiding in every waffle.
Beelzebub is a chocolate drop,
Lucifer is a lollipop.
Teach me the evils of hollandaise,
Of pasta and gobs of mayonnaise,
And crisp fried chicken from the South.
If You love me, Lord, shut my mouth.

—VIA REV. TOM WALSH, SCOTTSDALE, ARIZONA

Donald L. Cooper, M.D., of Stillwater, Oklahoma, who served on the President's Council on Physical Fitness and Sports, passed on the following story about a preacher who was on his deathbed:

The preacher called in his wife and children and said: "I know I'm terminal and don't have long to live. You'd better call my doctor and my lawyer. When I die, I want my doctor on my right and my lawyer on my left."

His wife called in the doctor and the lawyer, and when everyone was assembled around the deathbed, one of the children asked: "Dad, why do we have to have your doctor and lawyer here?"

"Christ died between two thieves, and I thought I'd do the same," the preacher said.

⑥

"Let my people go, or you will have to walk like that the rest of your life."

After a pastor's wife took her overworked husband to the family physician, the physician took the wife aside and whispered: "I don't like the way your husband looks."

"I don't either," she replied, "but he's always been a good father to the children."

—GEORGE GOLDTRAP, ORMOND-BY-THE-SEA, FLORIDA

"Heavy thoughts bring on physical maladies."
—Martin Luther

—VIA REV. NORMAN E. PORATH, SCHUYLER, NEBRASKA

Question: Can an atheist get insurance for acts of God?

—REV. KARL R. KRAFT, MANTUA, NEW JERSEY

Several women were visiting an elderly friend who was ill. After a while, they rose to leave and told her: "We will keep you in our prayers."

"Just wash the dishes in the kitchen," the ailing woman said. "I can do my own praying."

Headline in the December 1997 edition of *The Record*, publication of the Episcopal Diocese of Michigan:

"Bishop Richard Emrich Dies,
Returns to Michigan for Eternity."

—*THE ANGLICAN DIGEST*

There once was a deacon from Yuma
Who told a church joke to a puma.
Now his body lies
Under hot desert skies
For the puma had no sense of huma.

—VIA JOSEPH A. MAHER, OXNARD, CALIFORNIA

"A prominent doctor discovered that cheerful people resist disease better than chronic grumblers. He concluded that the surly bird gets the germ."

—LORIN D. WHITTAKER, M.D.,
LAUGH AWAY YOUR TENSIONS

From Zvi Kolitz's book The Teacher, *taken from the Talmud:*

Rabbi Beroka used to visit the marketplace, where the prophet Elijah often appeared to him. It was believed, as you know, that Elijah appeared to some saintly men to offer them spiritual guidance.

Once Rabbi Beroka asked the prophet, "Is there anyone here who has a share in the world to come?"

"No," the prophet replied.

While they were talking, two men passed them by. On seeing them, the prophet remarked, "These two men have a share in the world to come."

Rabbi Beroka then approached and asked them, "Can you tell me what is your occupation?"

"We are jesters," they replied. "When we see men depressed, we cheer them up."

The Billy Joe Wayne Ministries adopts a "hands-off" policy.

A doctor told a rich man that he would die in a couple of weeks. So the rich man called his three friends—the doctor, his pastor, and his lawyer—to his bedside. He said, "I am dying. My pastor has told me that I can't take it with me, but I think I've found a way. I have prepared three sealed envelopes, each containing ten thousand dollars in cash. When I die, I want each of you to walk by the casket and drop in your envelope with the ten thousand dollars."

After the funeral, the three friends met together. The preacher said, "I've got a confession to make. We needed to repair the church organ, so I took two thousand dollars out of my envelope and used it for the organ. I only dropped eight thousand dollars in my envelope."

The doctor confessed, "Well, I took five thousand dollars out for my new clinic and only dropped in five thousand dollars."

The lawyer said, "My conscience is clear. I did just what our good friend Joe asked. I kept my envelope, picked up both of yours, and dropped in a check for the full amount of thirty thousand dollars made out to Joe."

—VIA REV. LARRY LEA ODOM-GROH
FIRST CHRISTIAN CHURCH, CHILLICOTHE, MISSOURI

"**A Prayer:** I want to thank You, Lord, for being close to me so far this day. With Your help I haven't been impatient, lost my temper, been grumpy, judgmental or envious of anyone. But I will be getting out of bed in a minute, and I think I will really need Your help then. Amen."

—DEAN ALAN JONES
CHURCH OF THE RISEN CHRIST BULLETIN,
DENVER, COLORADO

AN ODE TO SICK WORSHIPERS

Barb Hughes lives in Portland, Oregon, with her husband, Chris, and their two children, Aubrey, four, and Toby, two. She wrote the editor of The Joyful Noiseletter: *"It seems every time my young family and I go to church, one of us gets sick." So she composed this "Ode to Sick Worshipers."*

> She loves little children,
> They're so darling and cute,
> But she's nursing a cold
> With a throat that's a beaut.
> She gushed as she touched
> Baby's hands and his cheeks.
> Now a haggard young mom
> Has sick babies for weeks.
>
> He's practiced and honed up
> His part in the choir

With the low bassy tones
And the melody higher.
His singing is splendid,
His harmony true,
But the choir won't appreciate
Sharing his flu.

Even "Miss Careful" who
Washes and lathers
Can't get away from
The sickness-germ-passers.
She's discovered the
Cleanest protection is fleeting
When shaking ill hands
During meeting and greeting.

You are a timely and
Needed church member,

In church every month—
As long as remembered.
But if your eyes or nose
Or your throat is so red,
You should be home,
With your tissues, in bed.

This sincere thought's
From a mom and a dad
And meant to protect us,
Our dear lass, and our lad.
We hope that you listen
To this little poem—
If you are sick, please
Be kind and *stay home!*

A pastor's wife called a veterinarian who makes house calls and told him her dog was very sick and wouldn't move. When the vet arrived, he found the dog on the floor with his feet in the air.

He examined the dog, but there was no response. He reached into his satchel, pulled out a live cat, moved the cat over the dog several times, and then put the cat back in his bag.

"I'm sorry, ma'am, but your dog is dead," the vet said. "That will be $430."

"Four hundred and thirty dollars! For what?" the woman exclaimed.

"The fee is thirty dollars for the house call and four hundred dollars for the CAT scan," the vet replied.

—VIA HENRY DOUGHTY, S. WOODSTOCK, CONNECTICUT

About a dozen years ago, the editor of *The Joyful Noiseletter*, the newsletter of the Fellowship of Merry Christians, received a letter from an unknown physician. The doctor said he used to be so deadly serious about everything that he once tried to kill himself; he then decided to commit himself to a mental hospital.

There, he said, he discovered the healing power of love, faith, and humor. After graduating from medical school, he said, he added another dimension to his medical practice by becoming a clown and humorist.

He said he also was organizing the Gesundheit Institute in Arlington, Virginia, with the aim of establishing a community of health professionals and patients "glued together by fun"— a new kind of hospital in the countryside of West Virginia.

"Fun," he wrote, "has overwhelmingly medicinal

effects on our patients. So many fewer pain medications! I am amazed at how humor has had a beneficial impact on disease, especially chronic disease such as arthritis and mental illness."

The physician became a member of the Fellowship, and from time to time through the years, *The Joyful Noiseletter* reported on the zany things he would do to get his patients to laugh.

He once dressed up in a white robe with angel's wings and went into a very sick and depressed patient's room and loudly proclaimed: "Previews of coming attractions!"

He used humor to attack the despair of potential suicides. "Many a suicide call to my office has begun with 'Doctor, I want to kill myself.' I just answer: 'Your place or mine?' The callers laugh, and I invite them over to talk."

He once sent out a fund-raising letter on behalf of the Gesundheit Institute that was written entirely in the Greek language. He later explained that he "gets so many fund-raising letters that they all start to look the same and they might as well be in Greek." He said he got a great response in donations to his Greek letter.

He passed on this quotation from the seventeenth-century English physician Dr. Thomas Sydenham: "The arrival of a good clown exercises more beneficial influence upon the health of a town than of twenty jackasses laden with drugs."

In 1998, Hunter ("Patch") Adams, M.D., finally received national attention. Comedian Robin Williams made him famous with his portrayal of "the clown-prince of physicians" in the movie *Patch Adams*.

"The trouble with many men is that they have got just enough religion to make them miserable. If there is not joy in religion, you have got a leak in your religion."

—BILLY SUNDAY, SERMON (1914)

Question: Why was Jesus born in a stable?
Answer: Mary and Joseph were enrolled in an HMO.

—REV. DANIEL L. ENGBER
ZION LUTHERAN CHURCH, BRISTOL, INDIANA

"The A.M.A. now says laughter is the best medicine."

ON GIVING THANKS

"I remember an elderly lady testifying that she had only two teeth left in her mouth (top and bottom), and she was 'rejoicing' because 'they hit.'"

—SHERWOOD ELIOT WIRT, *JESUS: MAN OF JOY*

The apostle Paul told the Philippians: "Forgetting what is behind and straining toward what is ahead, I press on toward the goal to win the prize…" The great philosopher Satchel Paige, may have been only paraphrasing him when he said: "Keep runnin' and don't look back, because somebody might be gainin' on you."

—JOE GARAGIOLA, *IT'S ANYBODY'S BALLGAME*

Rev. Warren J. Keating of the First Presbyterian Church in Derby, Kansas, told this story, which happened in the office of a family physician where Rev. Keating's wife works as a nurse:

A farm family—the mother along with her six-year-old son and three-year-old daughter—came to see the doctor because all three of them had been ill with the flu. The grandmother accompanied them.

The doctor explained that the mother and children needed to rest because they were sick.

"My grandma is sick too," the little boy said.

"No, your grandma is not sick," the doctor said.

"Oh, yes she is," the boy said. "She's depressed."

The mother added: "Yes, the children have been praying for their grandma and her depression."

The little boy turned to his grandma and said, "I'm

sorry to tell you this, Grandma, but you're going to be depressed for six more months."

"Why do you say that, honey?" his grandma asked.

"Well," the boy said, "I've been praying for a calf for six months and I just now got it!"

"Deadly" is a good adjective to use with "serious"; I've never heard the phrase "deadly humorous."

—LOIS GRANT PALCHES

"Show me a patient who is able to laugh and play, who enjoys living, and I'll show you someone who is going to live longer. Laughter makes the unbearable bearable, and a patient with a well-developed sense of humor has a better chance of recovery than a stolid individual who seldom laughs."

—BERNIE SIEGEL, M.D.

"Satchel [Paige], who pitched in the Major Leagues at the age of forty-eight, used to say, 'How old would you be if you didn't know how old you are?' I know twenty-year-old guys with ninety-year-old minds, and ninety-year-old guys with twenty-year-old minds."

—JOE GARAGIOLA, *IT'S ANYBODY'S BALLGAME*

"I heard you were here, Pastor, but I didn't want to cancel our counseling session."

© Steve Phelps

Rev. John J. Kelley, OMI, Catholic chaplain at the Deuel Vocational Institution in Tracy, California, collected these one-liners on the subject of giving advice:

- " 'Be yourself' is about the worst advice you can give to some people."
- "Advice is that which the wise don't need and the fool won't take."
- "The trouble with giving advice is that people want to repay you."
- "It's extremely difficult to take advice from some people when they need it more than you do."
- "The best advice: Say nothing often."

"Twenty-five percent of the people think the pastor can walk on water; twenty-five percent think he doesn't know enough to come in out of the rain; and fifty percent are satisfied if church is on time and the sermon isn't too long."

—MSGR. JOSEPH P. DOOLEY, MARTINS CREEK, PENNSYLVANIA

"I've always felt that people are better off looking ahead than looking back. Jack Benny felt the same way. 'The heck with the past,' he used to say."

—GEORGE BURNS AT AGE NINETY-FIVE

A melancholy man, always up on the latest accident and death statistics, once cornered Mark Twain. "Mr. Clemens," he said, "do you realize that every time I breathe an immortal soul passes into eternity?"

"Have you ever tried cloves?" Twain asked.

—REV. DENNIS R. FAKES, LINDSBORG, KANSAS

"If you want to keep happy and healthy, try being an 'inverse paranoid,'" says Dr. Rich Bimler, a Lutheran pastor, president of Wheat Ridge Ministries in Itasca, Illinois, and author of *Angels Can Fly Because They Take Themselves Lightly.*

"Try it. It works. Just imagine everyone you meet is trying to bring happiness and joy to your life. And then try to do the same for them."

Sign posted in a hospital ward:

> *NOTICE*
> *Due to the Current Budget Cutbacks,*
> *the Light at the End of the Tunnel*
> *Will Be Turned Off Until Further Notice*

—VIA LESLIE GIBSON-JOHNSON, RN,
PALM HARBOR, FLORIDA

Rev. Alfred Stangl, a chaplain at St. Cloud Hospital, tells this story:

"I remember one evening I visited a woman who was suffering from deep depression, to give her communion. But she was in the middle of a shower, so instead of drying her off, the nurse helped her slip on her robe. But first, so that the robe wouldn't get soaked, she draped her with newspapers.

"After I left and she resumed her shower, the imprint of the *St. Cloud Times* color comic section was all over her body like a tattoo. She and the nurse laughed so hard that she was discharged the next day, her depression as passé as yesterday's news."

—VIA JOSEPH YOUNG, *ST. CLOUD (MINNESOTA) VISITOR*

> "People with a sense of humor tend to be less egocentric. They are more humble in moments of success and less defeated in times of travail."
>
> —COMEDIAN BOB NEWHART

O ST. PETER, OPEN WIDE!

Monday I must make a salad
    For Circle Number Ten.
Tuesday, Bible study—
    It's our turn to serve again.
Wednesday night is Mariners—
    We're in charge of chili.
Children's choir on Thursday—
    "Please send cookies down with Willie."

Friday's U.P.W. —
    I'll take chocolate cake.
Saturday, check doughnut order
    For post-sermon coffee break.
Sunday eve is Fellowship—
    Pizza I must buy.
And although you see me smiling,
    There's more than meets the eye
Because, when day is over,
    I drop on bended knee.
I lift my voice to heaven
    And pray most fervently:
"O St. Peter up above,
    Those golden gates make wide
So that paunchy Presbyterians
    Can someday squeeze inside."

—DONA MADDUX COOPER, STILLWATER, OKLAHOMA

"No, Matilda, the Bible doesn't mention how may calories there were in a serving of manna."

> "Health and cheerfulness mutually beget each other. Laughter breaks the gloom which depresses the mind and dampens the spirit."
>
> —THOMAS ADDISON, M.D., ENGLISH PHYSICIAN (1793–1860)

"Last spring as I was getting ready to go into the city, the church janitor asked if I could stop at a hardware store and get him a vise grip. I had no idea what he really wanted, but I said I'd get it for him.

"The clerk at the store turned out to be a parishioner, so I asked him, 'Do you have any heavy-duty vises?'

"'Sorry, Father,' he said, 'I gave them all up for Lent.'"

—MSGR. CHARLES DOLLEN, *THE PRIEST*

When comedian Henny Youngman died at the age of ninety-one, hundreds of comics and friends paid tribute to him during his funeral at Riverside Memorial Chapel in Manhattan, the *Bergen Record* reported. Youngman was famous for his rapid-fire one-liners, including "Take my wife...please." After an effusive eulogy, Youngman's rabbi, Noach Valley of the Actor's Temple in New York, added: "Dear God, take Henny Youngman...please."

—BILL HANZALEK, RAMSEY, NEW JERSEY

"There is no beautifier of complexion, or form, or behavior like the wish to scatter joy—and not pain— around us."

—RALPH WALDO EMERSON

"Cheerfulness and contentment are great beautifiers and are great preservers of youthful looks."

—CHARLES DICKENS

A newly appointed bishop, received by Pope John XXIII in private audience, complained that the burden of his new office prevented him from sleeping. "Oh," said the pope, "the very same thing happened to me in the first few weeks of my pontificate. But then one day my guardian angel appeared to me in a daydream and whispered, 'Giovanni, don't take yourself so seriously. Try laughing at yourself.' And ever since then I've been able to sleep."

—EDWARD R. WALSH, WESTBURY, NEW YORK

William C. McVeigh and his wife, Ruth, who live in Fountain Hills, Arizona, have fourteen children. He tells this story about their "flood experience":

"When we were living in an old house in Jackson, Michigan, my wife was expecting our ninth child. The plumbing quite often sprung a leak, but the leaks could usually be easily fixed by wrapping cotton string over the spot and painting it with the residue from the bottom of a can of lead-based paint.

"I had just finished fixing a couple of leaks and was upstairs changing clothes when one of my daughters rushed up and told me the water burst. I dashed down to the basement, expecting to see water gushing from the spots I had repaired. I was relieved to find that all was well.

"I went back to the kitchen, where Ruth and the kids were gathered and assured them that everything was okay.

"Ruth said, '*My* water broke.'

"After a hurried trip to the hospital, son Joseph was born three hours later."

Irving Berlin, who lived to the age of 101, was a Jewish Russian immigrant who wrote nearly one thousand songs, including "God Bless America," "White Christmas," and "Easter Parade." Right up to the end, he never stopped making music. The aging composer once said: "The question is, 'Are you going to be a crabby old man or are you going to write another song?'"

A man fell into a pit and couldn't get himself out.

A *subjective* person came along and said, "I feel for you down there."

An *objective* person walked by and said, "It's logical that someone would fall down there."

A *Pharisee* said, "Only bad people fall into pits."

A *mathematician* calculated how he fell into the pit.

A *news reporter* wanted the exclusive story on the pit.

An *IRS agent* asked if he was paying taxes on the pit.

A *self-pitying* person said, "You haven't seen anything until you've seen my pit!"

A *fire-and-brimstone preacher* said, "You deserve your pit."

A *Christian Scientist* observed, "The pit is just in your mind."

A *psychologist* noted, "Your mother and father are to blame for your being in that pit."

A *self-esteem therapist* said, "Believe in yourself and you can get out of that pit."

An *optimist* said, "Things could get worse."

A *pessimist* claimed, "Things *will* get worse."

Jesus, seeing the man, took him by the hand and lifted him out of the pit.

—CHURCH BULLETIN IN AUSTRALIA

© 1994 Steve Phelps

"There were five first-time decisions, eight re-dedications, and 46 'That was the best rendition of Elijah's ascent in a flaming chariot I've ever seen.' All things considered, I'd say it was a great spring retreat."

© Steve Phelps

"It's important for your health to have an attitude of gratitude. When you get up in the morning, do you say, 'Good Lord, morning!'? Or do you say, 'Good morning, Lord!'?"

—GEORGE GOLDTRAP, ORMOND-BY-THE-SEA, FLORIDA

Deacon Sims comes down the aisle,
I wish Deacon Sims would smile.
Deacon Sims looks slightly bored—
Not like one who loves the Lord.

—LOIS GRANT PALCHES

FMC member Rev. J. Christy Ramsey, pastor of Ottawa (Ohio) Presbyterian Church, was asked by his personnel committee to evaluate his ministry in comparison to the ministry of Jesus. Here is Rev. Ramsey's humble response:

Jesus	Pastor Ramsey
Walks on water	Slips on ice
Changes water into wine	Changes water into coffee
Welcomes children	Has children's sermon
Curses fig tree	Kills houseplants
Stills the storm	Puts storm windows in sills
Feeds five-thousand	Buys snacks for youth groups
Sees Nathaniel under far-off tree	Watches world on CNN
Heals centurion's servant at distance	Can use TV remote control
Heals paralyzed man	Gets children to do chores

Jesus	Pastor Ramsey
Raises the dead	Wakes teenagers
Casts out demons	Turns on night-light
Overturns money-changers' tables	Puts away folding tables
Cleanses lepers	Has changed dirty diapers
Light of the world	Turner of light switches
Stands at door and knocks	Has church key
Calls disciples	E-mails session

ⓖ

"Thank you for waiting such a long time. You have the patience of Job, Mr....er...Job."

In a large Episcopal church in Virginia, the senior warden was addressing the congregation as he wrote on a blackboard: "MD, DD, LLD."

"Today," the warden said, "we welcome back our rector, who is returning from a sabbatical year during which he earned another college degree. For the information of you younger members, the letters on the blackboard stand for 'Mairzy doats and dozy doats and liddle lamzy divey.'"

—VIA BRUCE BURNSIDE, ROCKVILLE, MARYLAND

> *"Once again your cheeks will fill with laughter."*
>
> —Job 8:21 (THE JERUSALEM BIBLE)

"One of the tasks I had in our monastery was to go to the health care center, after our infirm sisters had finished their breakfast, and bring the food cart back to the main kitchen. Before returning, I would load any remaining food and/or dirty dishes on the cart. One morning a sister, noticing me put an empty platter on the cart, felt obliged to apologize, explaining: 'There's no coffee cake left.' I exclaimed with some indignation, 'Coffee cake…?! No, that was *stollen!*'

"Astonished, she responded, 'Oh really? That's too bad because we ate it all!'"

—SR. MARY E. PENROSE, OSB
ST. SCHOLASTICA MONASTERY, DULUTH, MINNESOTA

At the weekly Men in Motion luncheon at Central Baptist Church in Melbourne, Florida, the speaker was talking about the importance of forgiveness. He said, "The Lord has given me the command to forgive the wrongs of others, but He has not given me the ability to forget them."

From the back of the room, an older man interrupted the speaker: "Just wait a few years!"

—VIA PALMER STILES, MELBOURNE, FLORIDA

One priest was so frustrated over the failure of some in the pews to extend their hand at the sign of peace that he threatened to set up "Sign of Peace" and "No Sign of Peace" sections.

—DOLORES CURRAN, *ST. ANTHONY MESSENGER*

A traveling circuit rider loved a certain brand of extremely hot Tabasco sauce. He put it on everything he ate. When he traveled, he carried a small bottle of this sauce in a bag. One day the circuit rider stopped off in a small rural town. He went into the local restaurant and ordered a steak for lunch. When it was served, he pulled out his hot sauce, poured it on the steak, said grace, and began eating.

A salesman at the next table noticed how much the pastor was enjoying his meal.

"Say, Parson," said the salesman, "you seem to be really enjoying that steak."

"Why, yes, this is a very good steak," replied the minister, "but only because I added this special sauce on top."

"Could I give it a try?" asked the salesman.

"Of course," replied the minister, passing him the bottle. The salesman immediately applied a generous amount to his meal and took a bite.

"Sorry to bother you again, Pastor, but I have a question," said the salesman. "In your rounds do you often preach about hell?"

"Yes, I do," replied the circuit rider. "Why do you ask?"

The salesman replied, "Well, you're the first pastor I've ever met who carried samples of it with him."

—VIA REV. DAVID M. WADE
ST. PETER EVANGELICAL LUTHERAN CHURCH, SANTA
ANA, CALIFORNIA

"I have a friend who radiates joy, not because his life is easy, but because he habitually recognizes God's presence in the midst of all human suffering, his own as well as others. My friend's joy is contagious.

"The more I am with him, the more I catch glimpses of the sun shining through the clouds. While my friend always spoke about the sun, I kept speaking about the clouds, until one day I realized that it was the sun that allowed me to see the clouds.

"Those who keep speaking about the sun while walking under a cloudy sky are messengers of hope, the true saints of our day."

—HENRI NOUWEN

Col. Alexander K. McClure, a personal friend of Abraham Lincoln, said that "Lincoln's laugh was striking." McClure later published a book titled Abe Lincoln's Yarns and Stories. *Here is one of Lincoln's favorite stories:*

A minister and a lawyer were riding a train together.

"Sir," the minister asked the lawyer, "do you ever make mistakes while in court?"

"Very rarely," the lawyer said proudly, "but I must admit that, on occasion, I do."

"And what do you do when you make a mistake?" the minister asked.

"If they are large mistakes, I mend them," the lawyer said. "If they are small mistakes, I let them go. Tell me, Reverend, don't you ever make mistakes while preaching?"

"Of course," said the minister. "And I dispose of them in the same way that you do. Not long ago, I meant to tell the congregation that the devil was the father of liars, but I made a mistake and said the father of *lawyers*. The mistake was so small I let it go."

"Tonight we honor a man who gives new meaning to the phrase 'taking a moral stand.'"

© Ed Sullivan

"How necessary it is to cultivate a spirit of joy. To act lovingly is to begin to feel loving, and certainly to act joyfully brings joy to others, which in turn makes one feel joyful. I believe we are called to the duty of delight."

—DOROTHY DAY

"Religion will disappear."

—KARL MARX

"Karl Marx has disappeared."

—GOD

FMC member William Griffin is "a walking miracle," according to his pastor, Rev. David R. Francoeur, former rector of Christ Episcopal Church in Valdosta, Georgia.

When he was a colonel in the Air Force eighteen years ago, Griffin was involved in a terrible accident overseas. He was in a coma for a long time.

"In the early days of his recovery after he emerged from the coma, he couldn't communicate in any form but laughter," Rev. Francoeur said. "He tells me that he couldn't speak and his eyesight was poor, but he laughed a lot. I find this remarkable and told him that this is a sign of the healing work of the Holy Spirit. Today he is almost fully recovered."

Rev. Francoeur added: "The other day I was complaining to him about how God is so slow in answering prayer in comparison to the speed with which I think He should move. 'Why does God move so slowly?' I asked him.

"'Because He's older than you are,' he replied."

"Don't hang a dismal picture on the wall, and don't have gloom in your conversations. Don't be a cynic and disconsolate. Don't bewail and bemoan. Omit the negative propositions. Nerve us with incessant affirmatives. Don't waste yourself in rejection or bark against the bad, but chant the beauty of the good. Set down nothing that will not help somebody."

—RALPH WALDO EMERSON

"A number of years ago (before I was a member of FMC!), I was hospitalized for severe depression. One morning, while I was sitting on the edge of my bed and spilling buckets of tears, a lady came and sat next to me. Not knowing that I was a Christian, she held my hand and related the following to me:

" 'The world was never sadder than on Good Friday when Christ was crucified, but just three days later, the world was never brighter than when Christ rose from the grave. Whatever your problem is today, it will seem a lot less worrisome to you if you can wait just three days.'

"This lady was not a nurse, and when I inquired about her later, no one seemed to know who she may have been. (My guardian angel, perhaps?) I have clung to this thought for twelve years, and it has pulled me through many a trying time."

—EDITH CLOUD, JEFFERSONVILLE, PENNSYLVANIA

"An expectant woman is often called 'glowing and radiant.' It's really sweat."

—HUMORIST LIZ CURTIS HIGGS

"It is said that it's hard for churches in Arizona to motivate people with thoughts of the future life because it's so beautiful here in the winter that heaven has no attraction. And in the summer it's so hot here that hell doesn't scare them."

—FRED SEVIER, SUN CITY, ARIZONA

A man died and went to heaven. St. Peter escorted him past mansion after dazzling mansion until they came to a dilapidated shack at the end of the street.

The man was stunned and said, "St. Peter, why am I stuck with a rundown shack when all of these other people have mansions?"

"Well, sir," replied St. Peter, "we did the best we could with the money you sent us."

—RICK MOORE THE CRIMSON RIVER QUARTET,
MISSION VIEJO, CALIFORNIA

"You can't help getting older, but you don't have to get old."

—GEORGE BURNS AT HIS NINETY-FIFTH BIRTHDAY PARTY

"You're letting your refrigerator
lead you into temptation."

© Goddard Sherman

If you are on the Gloomy Line,
    Get a transfer.
If you're inclined to fret and pine,
    Get a transfer.
Get off the track of doubt and gloom,
Get on the Sunshine Track—there's room—
    Get a transfer.

If you're on the Worry Train,
    Get a transfer.
You must not stay there and complain,
    Get a transfer.
The Cheerful Cars are passing through,
And there's a lot of room for you—
    Get a transfer.

If you're on the Grouchy Track,
    Get a transfer.
Just take a Happy Special back,
    Get a transfer.
Jump on the train and pull the rope,
That lands you at the Station Hope—
    Get a transfer.

—ALBERT J. NIMETH, O.F.M.

"The way to cheerfulness is to keep our bodies in exercise and our minds at ease."

—RICHARD STEELE (1729)

"I live by this credo: 'Have a little laugh at life and look around you for happiness instead of sadness.' Laughter has always brought me out of unhappy situations. Even in your darkest moment, you usually can find something to laugh about if you try hard enough. If I can make people laugh, then I have served my purpose for God."

—RED SKELTON

TOP TEN REASONS WHY HEAVEN IS LOOKING GOOD

A cherished friend of Fred W. Sanford of Schaumburg, Illinois, battled cancer for years. "Several days before she died," Sanford said, "I thought the gift of humor would lift her up.

"As she lay on her couch and struggled to breathe, I told her I had a list called 'The Top Ten Reasons Why Heaven is Looking Good' and shared them with her:

10. You can begin the Lord's Prayer "Our Father, who art here…"

9. You can find out the answer to the question "Why?"

8. Wings

7. Soul music for eternity

6. Real golden arches

5. Great view

4. "No pain, no gain" becomes "No pain, no pain."

3. When you say, "Oh God…," you'll hear, "What?"

2. Harp lessons

1. Totally fat free

—FRED W. SANFORD. REPRINTED WITH PERMISSION.

"Have you done something to warrant a drive-by prayer group?"

© Ed Sullivan

Seen on a bulletin board at Mayo Clinic:

Cancer is limited.

It cannot cripple love.

It cannot shatter hope.

It cannot corrode faith.

It cannot eat away peace.

It cannot destroy confidence.

It cannot kill friendship.

It cannot shut out memories.

It cannot silence courage.

It cannot invade the soul.

It cannot reduce eternal life.

It cannot quench the Spirit.

It cannot lessen the power of the Resurrection.

—AUTHOR UNKNOWN
VIA PENNY MCBRIDE, DECATUR, ILLINOIS

"Some people just can't enjoy life: The first half of their lives are spent blaming their troubles on their parents and the second half on their children."

—Rev. Dennis R. Fakes, Lindsborg, Kansas

FMC member Jeanette Silva of Scott Bar, California, wears a button that declares:

"Warning: Humor may be hazardous to your illness."

Sign in the lobby of a Moscow hotel across from a Russian Orthodox monastery:

"You are welcome to visit the cemetery where famous Russian composers, artists, and writers are buried daily except Thursday."

—via Patty Wooten, Santa Cruz, California

Before Larry J. Crocker became minister of Marbach Christian Church in San Antonio, Texas, he was a funeral director. At one funeral, he recalls, he got his tie caught while closing a casket in front of twelve hundred people. "Needless to say," he says, "the decorum was lost, as was the tie."

On a trip to England, FMC member Susan Pellowe of Chicago visited her grandfather's grave in a Cornwall cemetery. She found this epitaph on the nearby tombstone of Samuel Carne, chosen by his widow, a friend of Susan's:

He Knew How to Smile

Rick Moore of the Crimson River Quartet, Mission Viejo, California, tells this true story:

A Southern Gospel group arrived home from a singing tour and was called by the widow of a man in their church who had just passed away. The widow asked them to sing three of her husband's favorite songs at the funeral: "In the Garden," "Amazing Grace," and "Jingle Bells."

The group leader had misgivings about singing "Jingle Bells" at a funeral, but when the widow insisted that her husband loved the song, he agreed to sing it, but told her that they would be singing it "real slow."

At the funeral service, the group sang all three songs, including "Jingle Bells," slowly and mournfully. Afterwards, the widow thanked the group for singing and added: "Oh, I remember the name of the song my husband liked so much. It wasn't 'Jingle Bells'; it was 'When They Ring Those Golden Bells.'"

Malcolm Muggeridge, a consulting editor to *The Joyful Noiseletter*, said he always derived great comfort from these lines by the English poet William Blake (1827):

> It is right it should be so;
> Man was made for joy and woe;
> And when this we rightly know
> Through the world we safely go.
> Joy and woe are woven fine,
> A clothing for the soul divine;
> Under every grief and pine
> Runs a joy with silken twine.

"We gather today to honor our youth pastor who died last Saturday from what the doctors are determining to be an overdose of cholesterol from eating too many pizzas."

© Dik LaPine

"When I was a child, my father was the pastor at Grace Lutheran Church in Rankin, Illinois. At one time he gave his sermon in Swedish at the first service and English at the second service.

"On Sunday he would leave early, and the job of getting five children to church on time was left to my mother and older sister. On one winter Sunday morning, colder than usual, we heard the order to be sure our shoes were shined.

"There was not time for shoe shining, so we grabbed the next best thing we could find for the job. It happened to be a large jar of Vicks VapoRub. We rubbed it on our shoes to a pretty good shine.

"Needless to say, the steam radiators in church were at their best that morning, and we cleared the heads of all the people in the pews."

—AL KARLSTROM, CHAMPAIGN, ILLINOIS

Sign in a funeral parlor:

> *"Ask about our layaway plan."*

> *"A good laugh heals a lot of hurts."*
> —MADELEINE L'ENGLE

Rev. Ronald J. Mohnickey, TOR, of the Holy Spirit Monastery at the Franciscan University of Steubenville, Ohio, celebrated Mass at a nearby church one hot summer morning. After the liturgy, a woman greeted him with a broad smile and said, "I am so happy when you celebrate Mass here!" Before Fr. Mohnickey could respond, she added, "When you come here, they always turn on the air conditioning because you sweat so much!"

"If you are to grow in good temper, you must grow in good humor. God has given us the power of laughter not only to laugh at things, but to laugh off things…. The art of laughing at yourself is the highest kind of laughter. Good humor will make you good-tempered.

"O Jesus, Thou wast 'anointed with the oil of gladness above Thy fellows.' Teach me Thy secret of holy laughter."

—E. STANLEY JONES, *GROWING SPIRITUALLY*
VIA PASTOR KEN KUBICHEK, DIAMOND, OHIO

"Trouble knocked at the door but, hearing laughter, hurried away."

—BEN FRANKLIN

ANTIDOTES FOR LOW SPIRITS

Some "Antidotes for Low Spirits" recommended in 1820 by Rev. Sydney Smith, an Anglican pastor.

- Go into the shower-bath with a small quantity of water at a temperature low enough to give you a slight sensation of cold—seventy-five or eighty degrees.
- Read amusing books.
- Be as busy as you can.
- See as much as you can of those friends who respect and like you, and of those acquaintances who amuse you.
- Avoid dramatic representations (except comedy) and serious novels.
- Do good.

- Do as much as you can in the open air without fatigue.
- Make the room where you commonly sit cheerful and pleasant.
- Struggle little by little against idleness.
- Be firm and constant in the exercise of rational religion.

"Jesus is the one who helped me smile, not because of my disability, but in spite of my disability."

—JONI EARECKSON TADA

My dad was an easygoing laid-back type of guy, so much so that Mom often told him that he would be late for his own funeral.

When Dad passed away, he *was* late for his own wake because of a mix-up between the hospital and the funeral home. So Mom sat in an office chair at the funeral home and laughed.

We opted to display an empty, closed casket for family and friends at the wake. One gentleman could not understand why the casket was closed.

Unable to avoid his insistent questions, I finally took him aside. "Because it's empty," I whispered.

"Ooooooh!" he said, still nodding his head. "Well, where's your father?"

"He's still at the hospital," I replied.

"Ooooooh!" he said, still nodding his head. "Aren't you rushing things a bit?"

When my mom passed away, her funeral also had its own little twist.

One of her favorite sayings was, "If _____ saw or heard that, they'd roll over in their grave." Well, wouldn't you know that during her funeral, the pallbearers stumbled, causing Mom to roll over onto her side.

Even in the most tragic of circumstances, laughter can ease much of the pain of loss.

My parents, Leo and Rose, have been with Jesus for some time now, but they still manage to make us laugh. May you both rest in the peace, love, joy, and laughter of our Lord.

—FMC MEMBER JAMES J. REYOR, SR.,
SPRINGFIELD, MASSACHUSETTS

During an examination, a rookie police officer was asked what strategy he would use to disperse a threatening crowd.

"I would take up a <u>collection</u>," he wrote.

—VIA CATHERINE HALL, PITTSBURGH, PENNSYLVANIA

The solemn saints discourage
Many folk from being good,
While this gaiety of sinners
Makes more converts than it should.

—LOIS GRANT PALCHES, CONCORD, MASSACHUSETTS

Annoyed by complaints from some parishioners that incense used during Mass was choking them, the pastor of Our Lady of Mt. Carmel Church in Niles, Ohio, placed the following announcement in the church bulletin:

> "Please Note: For our liturgical celebrations, a *non-choking* incense will be used."

(Fr. John Trimbur, of St. John the Baptist Catholic Church in Campbell, Ohio, passed on this item with the comment that he doubted whether a "non-choking incense" is on the market. But Linda Raden, a secretary in a Catholic diocese, reported that "we use a chokeless incense at our cathedral in Gaylord, Michigan.")

"Well, I guess this leaves only taxes as being for certain."

© Dik LaPine

"The devil is most happy when he can snatch from a servant of God true joy of the Spirit. He carries dust with him to throw into the smallest chinks of conscience and thus soil one's mental candor and purity of life. But if joy of the Spirit fills the heart, the serpent shoots his deadly venom in vain."

—St. Francis of Assisi

"In Nigeria, the name of God is 'Father of Laughter.'"

—Joseph R. Veneroso, *Maryknoll* magazine

Ann Weeks is a nurse family therapist in Louisville, Kentucky. The following story is reprinted, with permission, from her book She Laughs and the World Laughs with Her.

One of the many challenges that I was confronted with after my first husband's death was people calling and asking to speak to him. Paul was an attorney, and calls from clients and others unaware of his death continued for weeks.

One evening a couple of months after Paul's death, the phone rang. "Hello, Kleine-Krachts' residence," I stated.

"May I speak to Paul Kleine-Kracht?" a man asked. I caught my breath and said, "I'm sorry, Paul is deceased. I'm his wife. May I help you?"

Without any comment about what I'd just said, the caller jumped right in with "I'm John Jones with the

Appliance Warranty Center. I'm calling to remind you that your warranty on your appliance is about to expire and you need to renew it."

"Thank you for calling, but that appliance is several years old and I've decided not to renew the warranty," I said.

With a tone of impatience, he responded, "Well, I'm sure your dead husband would want you to renew."

My humor and coping mechanism clicked in, and I replied, "Funny you should mention it, but just hours before Paul died he said, 'Honey, whatever you do, don't renew the appliance warranty!'"

There was silence and then John Jones said, "Oh…oh…okay," and hung up.

⊚

Rev. John Riley, rector of All Saints Episcopal Church, Jacksonville, Florida, passed on this story:

Following the funeral of a very prominent church person, the family left the church and began to form the funeral procession to the cemetery. The funeral director carefully instructed the parishioners on which car was to follow which car.

A motorcycle escort led about thirty cars to the cemetery. About four blocks from the cemetery's main gate, the driver of the fourth car suddenly decided that he was hungry and wanted to stop off at his nearby home for lunch.

When the driver made a right turn onto his street, twenty-five cars behind him in the procession followed him.

At the graveside, the funeral director, the family of the deceased, and Rev. Riley wondered what had happened to everyone. Due to time limits in the cemetery, the committal was read and the blessing given. It was not until the next day that they discovered that one friend of the deceased had an enormous gathering at his home for lunch.

"Fear can paralyze and even kill people. Fear, like misery, loves company. Faith and laughter are Fear's most formidable foes. Laughter cuts Fear down to size. Fear takes itself so seriously, but it shrinks when we laugh in its face. Poke fun at Fear and it goes into a frenzy. Why not resolve in this new millennium to laugh at Fear?"

—HUMORIST PEGGY GOLDTRAP, ORMOND-BY-THE-SEA, FLORIDA

"You worry too much, Noah. You've got to accentuate the positive, eliminate the negative, latch on to the affirmative, and don't mess with Mister In-between."

Grace Episcopal Church of Jefferson City, Missouri, hosted its second annual "No Excuse Sunday," with the following props provided to anticipate any excuse for not attending church:

"Blankets and sweaters for those who don't come because the church is too cold; fans for those who stay away because it is too warm; hard hats for those who are afraid the roof will fall in; stopwatches and whistles for those who think the sermons are too long; cushions for those who think the pews are too hard; and name tags for those who are afraid they won't be recognized."

The church also announced it would provide free transportation.

—VIA FRANK W. WAY, JEFFERSON CITY, MISSOURI

Not even approaching death could erase Winston Churchill's keen sense of humor. Churchill planned his own funeral and filled it with the promise of Easter. After the benediction, he directed that a bugle high up in the dome of St. Paul's Cathedral would play "Taps." Churchill then directed that immediately after the playing of "Taps," a second bugler, also in the dome, would play "Reveille," a call to get up in the morning.

"A good laugh and a long sleep are the two best cures."

—IRISH PROVERB

"Old preachers never die; they just get put out to pastor."

—PASTOR DAVE BUUCK, CAMBRIDGE, MINNESOTA

A pastor was called to a local nursing home to perform a wedding. An anxious old man met him at the door. The pastor sat down to counsel the old man and asked several questions. "Do you love her?"

The old man replied, "Nope."

"Is she a good Christian woman?"

"I don't know for sure," the old man answered.

"Does she have lots of money?" asked the pastor.

"I doubt it."

"Then why are you marrying her?" the preacher asked.

"'Cause she can drive at night," the old man said.

—GEORGE GOLDTRAP, ORMOND-BY-THE-SEA, FLORIDA

For many years, FMC member Rev. Tom Walsh of Scottsdale, Arizona, has taught a course called "Humor, Hilarity, Healing, and Happy Hypothalami."

"If God the Father saw fit to clothe His Son in a human body, that makes the body sacred," says Walsh. "So when we take care of that body by diet, exercise, prayer, laughter—especially laughter at ourselves—we give glory to God."

Long ago, Walsh befriended humorist Erma Bombeck when they were both at St. Thomas the Apostle Church in Scottsdale. Walsh asked Bombeck if she thought humor was healing.

"I suspect you have me confused with Norman Cousins," Bombeck wrote Walsh. "He's several inches taller, and he laughed his way through illness. He got a best-seller out of his illness. I got three children. Those are the breaks.

"I am a great believer in your premise that humor heals. I have nothing to back it up physically, but I have file drawers of pure testimonials."

Bombeck once wrote a column about heaven in which she speculated that "it's probably just one big *Jeopardy!* game in the sky, where all day long you struggle to remember names."

"Faith can turn trials into triumphs and gloom into gladness."

—WINSTON CHURCHILL

"I've heard reports about ministerial burn-out, but this is the first time I've actually seen one."

© Dennis Daniel

Roseann Alexander-Isham of Eugene, Oregon, wrote to the editor of *The Joyful Noiseletter:* "I suffer from occasional bouts of depression. But each day I decide to be happy, and look for the small joys, and do something good for someone else if possible. I put a smile on my face and 'act as if until it becomes.' And it works most of the time. One day when I was in the pits, I asked myself, 'What should I pray for?' I composed a prayer and would like to share it with you."

Here is Roseann's prayer:

> "Lord, grant me a joyful heart and a holy sense of humor. Please give me the gift of faith to be renewed and shared with others each day. Teach me to live this moment only, looking neither to the past with regret nor to the future with apprehension. Let love be my aim and my life a prayer."

TOP TEN REASONS FOR JOINING THE CHURCH CHOIR

10. The collection plate is never passed to the choir.

9. You want to be near the pastor when he preaches in case he says anything heretical.

8. When you forget to do your laundry, the choir robes cover dirty clothes.

7. You want to make sure you always have a seat in church.

6. The chairs in the choir are more comfortable than the chairs in the pews.

5. You can see everyone who is in church and they can see you.

4. The pastor won't see you if you take a short nap.

3. You want to get used to sitting with a group of people in case you're selected for jury duty.

2. Your favorite movie is "The Preacher's Wife."

1. You'll be the first to know when it's twelve noon
    because you can see the clock in the rear of the
    sanctuary.

> —VIA REV. H. WARREN CASIDAY
> EMANUEL UNITED CHURCH OF CHRIST,
> THOMASVILLE, NORTH CAROLINA

The phrase that is guaranteed to wake up an audience:
"And in conclusion."

> —CHARLES J. MILAZZO, ST. PETERSBURG, FLORIDA

"Today may the sun shine on your world;
may the rain fall on your garden;
may the clouds pass over your troubles;
may the stars twinkle on your life;
may the moon brighten your journey;
and may tonight bring you a better tomorrow."
                    —*Old Irish Blessing*

—VIA REV. JOHN H. FAHEY, WASHINGTON,
WEST VIRGINIA

"I will have no melancholy or sad spirits in my house.
Persevere in cheerfulness, for this is the true way to make
progress in virtue."

—PHILIP NERI (1515–1595)

A sure sign your pastor is ready
for a vacation.

© Steve Phelps

THE GIFT

Sense of humor—God's great gift—
Causes spirits to uplift;
Helps to make our bodies mend;
Lightens burdens; cheers a friend;
Tickles children; elders grin
At this warmth that glows within;
Surely in the Great Hereafter
Heaven must be full of laughter!

—ELEANOR DAVIES, MEADVILLE, PENNSYLVANIA

A zealous man once telephoned Woodrow Wilson in the wee hours of the morning when Wilson was governor of New Jersey, rousing him from sleep. "Governor Wilson," the man announced, "your commissioner of highways just died, and I would like to take his place."

"If it's all right with the undertaker, it's all right with me," Wilson replied.

—PASTOR VIGGO ARONSEN, KERRVILLE, TEXAS

"Our theology should enable us to see God as one in whom we can trust, even in the middle of the ultimate fear which is death. If we can laugh in the crisis of death, that's one way of saying that God is in charge."

—HUMORIST TOM MULLEN

A florist's new assistant took a telephone order from a customer. "The ribbon must be white," said the woman on the phone, "with gold letters reading 'Rest in Peace' on both sides. And, if you can squeeze it in, 'We Shall Meet in Heaven.'"

When the floral tribute reached the home of the deceased, the inscription read:

Rest in Peace on Both Sides!
If You Can Squeeze in,
We Shall Meet in Heaven!

—*Liguorian*

"In my synagogue, somber is for the dead. My philosophy is that religion ought to be something enjoyable."

—Rabbi Jack Segal, Beth Yeshurun Synagogue,
Houston, Texas, the *Dallas Morning News*

Sure, it cost more, but Pastor Lou enjoyed staying home while sending the *congregation* on vacation.

DIETER'S PRAYER #2

The Lord is my shepherd, I shall not want.

He maketh me lie down and do push-ups,

He giveth me sodium-free bread,

He restoreth my waistline,

He leadeth me past the refrigerator for mine own
sake.

He maketh me partake of broccoli instead of potatoes,

He leadeth me past the pizzeria.

Yea, though I walk through the bakery

I shall not falter, for Thou art with me.

With diet colas I am comforted.

Though preparest a diet for me in the presence of
my enemies,

Thou anointest my lettuce with low-cal olive oil.

My cup will not overflow.

Surely Ry-Krisp and D-Zerta shall follow me all the
days of my life,
And I shall live with the pangs of hunger forever.
Amen.

—AUTHOR UNKNOWN

"The sadnesses of life—far from totally discouraging
laughter—give rise to it."

—STEVE ALLEN

"If you, O Servant of God, are upset, for any reason whatever, you should immediately rise up to prayer, and you
should remain in the presence of the Most High Father
for as long as it takes for Him to restore to you the joy of
your salvation."

—ST. FRANCIS OF ASSISI

"God does not insist or desire that we should mourn in agony of heart; rather it is His wish that out of love for Him, we should rejoice with laughter in our soul."

—JOHN CLIMACUS (A.D. 649)

"God is not a God of sadness, death, etc., but the devil is. Christ is a God of joy, and so the Scriptures often say that we should rejoice.... A Christian should and must be a cheerful person."

—MARTIN LUTHER

"Sour godliness is the devil's religion."

—JOHN WESLEY

"What do you think of the video I made of your sermon last Sunday?"

"I saw the Lord scorn the devil's malice and reduce his powerlessness to nothing, and He wills that we do the same thing. On account of this sight, I laughed out loud and long, which made those who were around me laugh, too, and their laughter was a pleasure to me.

"Then I thought I would like all my fellow Christians to have seen what I saw, for then they should all laugh with me. For I understood that we may laugh, comforting ourselves and rejoicing in God that the devil has been overcome."

—DAME JULIAN OF NORWICH
FOURTEENTH-CENTURY ENGLISH MYSTIC

"Cana of Galilee…Ah, that sweet miracle! It was not men's grief, but their joy Christ visited. He worked His first miracle to help men's gladness."

—FYODOR DOSTOEVSKY

"A person without a sense of humor is like a wagon without springs, jolted by every pebble in the road."

—HENRY WARD BEECHER

"Were it not for my little jokes, I could not bear the burdens of this office…With the fearful strain that is on me night and day, if I did not laugh I should die."

—ABRAHAM LINCOLN

"To forgive heals the wound; to forget heals the scar."

—P. T. BARNUM

"I could not be interested in any man's religion if his knowledge of God did not bring him more joy, did not brighten his life, did not make him want to carry this joy into every dark corner of the world. I have no understanding of a long-faced Christian. If God is anything, He must be Joy!"

—COMEDIAN JOE E. BROWN

"If a fellow doesn't have a good time once in a while and get a good laugh out of the serious side of life, he doesn't half live."

—WILL ROGERS

"I think it is impossible to live and not to grieve, but I am always suspicious of my own grief lest it be self-pity in sheep's clothing. Altogether it is better to pray than to grieve; and it is greater to be joyful than to grieve. But it takes more grace to be joyful than any but the greatest have."

—FLANNERY O'CONNOR

"Don't live in the past. Don't live in the future. This is the moment God has given us to be useful."

—FULTON SHEEN

"God forgets the past; imitate Him."

—MAX LUCADO

"Christian men are but men. They may have a bad liver, or an attack of bile, or some trial, and then they get depressed if they have ever so much grace. But what then? Well, then you can get joy and peace through believing. I am the subject of depressions of spirit so fearful that I hope none of you ever gets to such extremes of wretchedness as I go to. But I always get back again by this: I know I trust Christ. I have no reliance but in Him. Because He lives, I shall live also, and I spring to my legs again and fight with my depressions of spirit and my downcast soul and get the victory through it. So may you do, and so you must, for there is no other way of escaping from it. In your most depressed seasons, you are to get joy and peace through believing."

—CHARLES SPURGEON
NINTEENTH-CENTURY ENGLISH BAPTIST PASTOR

If you enjoyed this gift book, ask for the others at your local bookstore…

Mirth for the Millennium, ISBN: 1-57856-283-X

From the Mouths of Babes, ISBN: 1-57856-284-8

Rolling in the Aisles, ISBN: 1-57856-285-6

…as well as the full-length paperbacks from which they were drawn:

Holy Humor, ISBN: 1-57856-279-1

More Holy Humor, ISBN: 1-57856-280-5

Holy Hilarity, ISBN: 1-57856-281-3

More Holy Hilarity, ISBN: 1-57856-282-1

WATERBROOK
PRESS